Make a Christmas Memory

Simple Things You Can Do to Celebrate the True Meaning of Christmas

Julaine Kammrath

Illustrated by Michelle Dorenkamp

SAINT LOUIS

For Lara, Matt, and Barbara, fellow travelers

Designed by Karen Pauls and Jennifer Horton.

Scripture taken from the HOLY BIBLE, NEW INTERNATIONAL VERSION®. NIV®. Copyright © 1973, 1978, 1984 by International Bible Society. Used by permission of Zondervan Publishing House. All rights reserved.

Copyright © 1996 Concordia Publishing House
3558 S. Jefferson Avenue, St. Louis, MO 63118-3968
Manufactured in the United States of America

2 3 4 5 6 7 8 9 10 11   06 05 04 03 02 01 00 99 98 97

CONTENTS

INTRODUCTION

You and your family will enjoy using this book to create Christmas memories you will treasure all your lives. If you wish, you can use a different story or activity each day through Advent, Christmas, and the 12 days of Christmas. Many of the activities will involve pieces from a créche set. If you do not have a family créche set, or if your set is breakable, use the figures in the back of book. As Advent begins, help your children cut them out to make stand-up figures. You may wish to make a stable from a box. To complete the projects in this book, first photocopy the patterns or trace them onto paper.

As you read and enjoy *Make a Christmas Memory*, help your children find the little lost lamb that wanders through the book. Gather around the manger to celebrate God's gift of His Son to be our Savior and build a lifetime of Christmas memories.

GIFT GIVING

Put the Baby Jesus from your crèche set, or a small baby doll, inside a box and wrap it in colorful paper. Label the box *To: You. From: God.* Let your child unwrap it before reading the comments below.

Do you know who invented the idea of presents at Christmas? God did! Baby Jesus was God's first Christmas present. Of course, God was giving presents all along—rainbow flowers that color springtime, strong trees for climbing, water-polished pebbles, the smell of bread baking. Can you name more gifts that God gives us? Think about your five senses as you name things.

God gives us many presents all the time. At Christmas we remember the *very best Gift* of all—Jesus, the Son of God, born into our world to be our Savior. That special present is what Christmastime is all about!

Make a Christmas Memory

★ Draw some of the presents you named on self-stick notes. Stick them under a paper Christmas tree on the refrigerator. You might add Baby Jesus too!

★ Use this book as a calendar each December. Select 24 or more—you may want to begin your activities on the first Sunday in Advent—activities. Write their numbers on slips of paper and wrap them. Hang these tiny presents on a Christmas tree or set them among the greenery of an Advent wreath. Each day during Advent, ask a family member to pick a present. Look up the activity and do it together. Be sure you have all the materials needed on hand. Our family of five has done this for more than 10 years, and the tradition has made Advent a joyful time that focuses on Jesus.

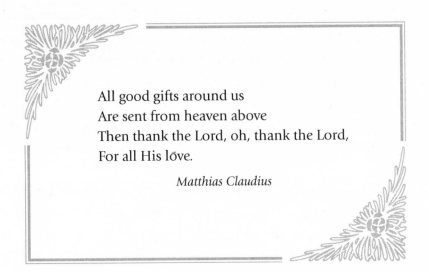

All good gifts around us
Are sent from heaven above
Then thank the Lord, oh, thank the Lord,
For all His love.

Matthias Claudius

SWADDLING CLOTHES

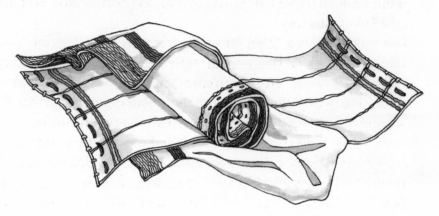

Mary didn't know that the birth of her baby would start a celebration that we now look forward to with such delight. But she did prepare for the special day in her own way. Jewish women made swaddling clothes, strips of cloth often lovingly embroidered, to wrap around their babies. Mary probably rolled them up and tucked them in her bag when she and Joseph started off to Bethlehem. As Mary touched them, she must have thought how they would hug the little boy now kicking inside her womb. The swaddling strips would make Baby Jesus feel cuddled, even when He lay sleeping.

Did you have a special blanket or lovey when you were small? What do you remember about it? Ask older children what we might learn about God because He included the swaddling clothes in the biblical account of Christmas. He chose to tell us about them. Why?

Make a Christmas Memory

★ Cut cloth strips and decorate them with markers. Wrap a baby doll in them just as Mary wrapped Baby Jesus in swaddling clothes.

★ To Jesus, swaddling clothes were like hugs from people who loved Him. Play a hugging game. Get an empty soda bottle and lay it sideways in the center of your family circle. Take turns spinning it. Whomever the bottle points to gets a hug from the spinner! Keep spinning until everyone's had plenty of hugs.

★ Just for fun, use toilet paper to wrap Mom or Dad in swaddling clothes. What tiny animal does God wrap in "swaddling clothes"?   *(The silkworm.)*

★ Make stollen, a German yeast bread that resembles a child wrapped in swaddling.

1 pkg. dry yeast	½ cup butter
¾ cup warm water	3½ cups flour (separated)
½ cup sugar	½ cup chopped almonds
½ tsp. salt	¼ cup raisins or other dried fruit
3 eggs	

Mix yeast and warm water. Wait 5 minutes. Add sugar, salt, eggs, butter, and 1½ cups flour. Beat 10 minutes. Stir in 2 cups flour, almonds, and raisins or other dried fruit. Cover and let rise one hour. Beat down. Cover and refrigerate at least 8 hours. Divide dough into three portions. Roll each portion into a rope. Braid the ropes and lay them on a cookie sheet. Squeeze and tuck the dough to look like a swaddled baby. Let rise one hour. Heat oven to 375°. Mix 1 egg yolk with ¼ teaspoon water and brush on top of dough. Bake 20 minutes.

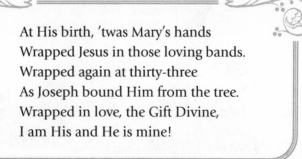

At His birth, 'twas Mary's hands
Wrapped Jesus in those loving bands.
Wrapped again at thirty-three
As Joseph bound Him from the tree.
Wrapped in love, the Gift Divine,
I am His and He is mine!

BETHLEHEM YARN BALL

"Drop by me," Erika breathed. She watched the yarn ball unroll toward her brother. Mike gripped the yarn with one hand and pushed the rest of the ball toward Mother.

Erika's eyes glistened. No prize dropped out! Mother smiled as she pushed the unwinding ball toward Erika.

Slowly it turned over and over. Just before reaching Erika's place, a tiny packet plopped down. Erika jumped up from her chair and grabbed it.

"Mommie, I got it!"

"Open it carefully."

Erika unwrapped a shiny dime and read the card with it. Her family talked a bit and then listened to Mike read from Luke 2, up to the new verse number written on the packet.

Later, Mother cut the yarn so that tomorrow the ball could be unrolled around the table again until the next packet fell out in front of someone. As Mom put things away, Erika wondered aloud, "Who will get the present next?"

Mom grinned. "It will be a surprise—another one from God."

Erika followed Mother to the sink. "What do you mean *another* surprise?"

"God has hidden surprises in our whole lives. He planned for us before we were even born."

Erika drew her eyebrows together. "God *planned* us?"

"Uh-hum. It's like when I made the Bethlehem ball. I put the surprises in one at a time, winding and winding the yarn. I planned that each surprise would come after some yarn had unraveled. God planned talents and blessings to appear in our lives, popping out every once in a while as we grow older.

Erika thought a minute. "You mean like when I was six and I won the coloring contest?"

"Yes, and other things too. When you were four God surprised us with your talent for making jokes. This year I think God may have tucked in a good-gymnast talent." Mother put a soapsud on Erika's nose. "As time unrolls, we'll see what other surprise talents God put in you!"

Erika brushed the foam off her nose and did a cartwheel on the tile floor.

"I think you're unraveling, Erika!" Mother laughed.

Make a Christmas Memory

★ Make a Bethlehem yarn ball. Label and wrap the packets, placing a card with the verse numbers from Luke 2:1–20 and discussion items, as described, with each one. Wind yarn around the last packet (verses 17–20). When it's covered, lay the next to last packet on the ball. Keep winding yarn until it is secure. Continue in this way until the ball is big and lumpy! Unwind it every other day like Erika's family did. You can use this ball of yarn every day of December until Christmas by adding four small candles and the items listed on page 39. Arrange for the candles to fall out on Sundays and use them to light your Advent wreath.

Verses 1–2: *Coin.* Explain how taxation works now.

Verse 3: *Birth certificate.* Where were each of you born?

Verse 4: *Picture of grandparents.* King David was Joseph's great, great, great, … grandfather. Share family memorabilia!

Verse 5: *Balloon.* God made mothers' wombs stretchy like balloons so babies can grow. What does Mom remember about being "with child"?

Verses 6–7: *NO VACANCY sign.* What is the difference between sleeping in a motel and sleeping in a garage? How do the differences compare to sleeping in an inn and a stable?

Verse 8: *Candy cane.* A candy cane is shaped like the staff that shepherds use. What do they use staffs for?

Verse 9: *Card that says, "Get flashlight."* Shine the flashlight behind someone's head and imagine a little bit of the "glory of the Lord."

Verses 10–12: *Small magnifying glass.* What two clues did the angel give the shepherds?

Verses 13–14: *Paper-doll angels.* Unfold these as you sing "Angels We Have Heard on High."

Verses 15–16: *Card that says, "Get some running shoes."* Why did the shepherds run?

Verses 17–20: *Paper megaphone.* What do you think the shepherds said to the villagers? How can we tell someone about Baby Jesus right now?

• •

Sing a favorite Christmas carol.

No Room

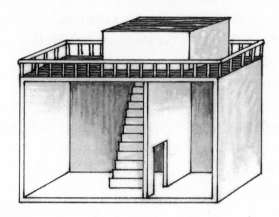

"Get that, will you!" the innkeeper shouted over the noise of the newest arrivals. Six people, six people, where can I put this group? he thought as they climbed the steps to the roof.

A knock rapped on the door again.

"Martha! See to the door!" the flustered man called over his shoulder. "Here, let me carry that," he said. The woman in the lead handed over a bundle of what smelled like barley bread and goat cheese and reached for her toddler, who'd stumbled. She looked so weary. The father cast a worried glance upward.

"Yes, I'm full to bursting, but if you're willing to spread out right by the top of the steps, you'll at least have a safe place to sleep. You register for taxes in the morning, and with the Lord's goodness, you can head home tomorrow afternoon. We've never had so many travelers in our little town of Bethlehem before."

For the third time there came an insistent knock on the door. The innkeeper peered past the family on the steps into the inn's main room. Groups with their small animals, goats and chickens, stuffed the room. Martha was pushing the water pot over to the corner to make room for a large family. "Here now. Put your things here. I'll just get the door," the innkeeper said.

Squeezing between two of the boys on the narrow steps, the innkeeper picked his way down and over a group of eight at the bottom to get to the door. He opened it on a large man, obviously in some sort of trade, and his very pregnant wife.

"Do you have room for us?" the man asked. "We've traveled three days from Nazareth."

The innkeeper looked at the center of the steps, the only clear space. A pregnant woman can't sleep there, he thought. "I'm sorry. I have no room, my friend."

The woman lowered her head and looked away. The innkeeper, a good man, saw her distress. He thought quickly. "But there is a stable outside. At least it would be fairly flat, and you can get clean straw."

The big man nodded his thanks. "The Lord bless you," the innkeeper called as they walked to the stable.

The woman turned and smiled gently. "He has," she whispered.

Make a Christmas Memory

★ This story is told from the innkeeper's point of view. Pass out the créche pieces. Ask, "How would you tell the Bethlehem story if you were this person or object?"

★ Using the illustration on page 15 as a guide, make an inn from a shoe box. Play out the story with your créche set.

 16

★ Shut all the inside doors of your home. Let Daddy, Mommy, or a big brother or sister be the donkey giving Joseph or Mary rides as they travel to Bethlehem. Knock on the "inn doors" and have someone open each to sadly say, "No room." Take turns playing the different roles.

★ In Mexico, Christians traditionally go from house to house playing out the "no room" drama. At each house, the carolers ask for room and after hearing "No room!" receive various cookies and treats. Consider asking church friends and neighbors to share this *Posada* custom with your family this year.

• •

Ask Jesus, "Make my heart a peaceful place for You to stay."

CHRISTMAS CLUE GAME

"So what clues did the angel give the shepherds?" Mother asked. Both older girls tried to out-shout each other with the answer. "Let David tell," Mother said as she hushed the other two.

"I can't remember," David answered.

"Listen closely for it when we read the Bible again tomorrow," Mother said as she fondly looked at her six-year-old. Then she turned to Yvonne and Rachel. "Would you like to play the Christmas clue game?"

Squeals of delight answered the question. They'd played this game once before, so the girls knew just what to do. Hands reached for the first clue paper from Mother. Yvonne read, "To get on the trail of clues, look for something musical."

Yvonne sucked in her lip and stared at the ceiling while David dashed over to the tape player. Rachel searched under the music box.

"You have to think harder than that," Mom teased.

Yvonne snapped her fingers. "I've got it!" She headed for the kitchen, and the others followed. Carefully, she lifted the lid of the teapot.

"That was a good guess. It sings one note, but the clue isn't there," said Mom.

"I see it!" shouted David, reaching for the folded paper stuck to the side of the telephone. He unfolded it as his sisters' heads bent over his. It said, *Congratulations, you're on the trail! Now look for something that gives Light to everyone.*

All three children began checking under various lamps, candles, and Christmas lights in the house. "I didn't put it on the ceiling, if that's what you're wondering," said Mother after they'd searched a while.

"But we've checked every lamp, Mom. Can't you give us a hint?"

Just then Shawn walked out of his bedroom, so Mom pulled him onto her lap. "Okay. *Light* starts with a capital *L* in this clue."

No one moved. Then Rachel raced off to the living room. "It's here!" she called. She pulled the paper from behind the picture of Jesus.

Shawn clapped his hands. "One more to go!" shouted David.

"I'll read it!" Rachel said as Yvonne tried to take the clue. Yvonne turned around and crossed her arms over her chest. "Your trail of clues ends with something Jesus didn't have," Rachel read out loud.

"Mom, Jesus didn't have lots of things—no toys or TV or books or anything."

"Think harder. Jesus had toys His earthly dad, Joseph, made. And He had books too—scrolls."

Baby Christi made a noise from her bedroom. Suddenly Rachel's face lit up. "I know!"

"Don't wake her up!" Mother called. Rachel immediately began to tip-toe and came back shortly with the last clue.

"It was on the crib," she said with a grin. She handed the riddle to Yvonne, who read, "You've followed the clues. Can you guess the riddle? I'm a créche piece. I'm young. I can get lost so I need watching."

Yvonne smiled. She walked over to the manger set and picked up a piece. She carried it back in her closed hand. Can you guess what was in her hand? *(The lamb.)*

Make a Christmas Memory

★ Play the Christmas clue game at your house. Take turns making up clues and solving the final riddle.

★ "10 Questions" is another type of clue game. The first player decides on a person, place, or thing from the Christmas story. The rest ask yes-or-no questions. If someone guesses the answer correctly by the 10th question, that person gets to start the game again.

• •

Say this Bible verse together each day for a week until you memorize it:

Ask and it will be given to you; seek and you will
find; knock and the door will be opened to you.
(Matthew 7:7)

St. Nicholas' Day

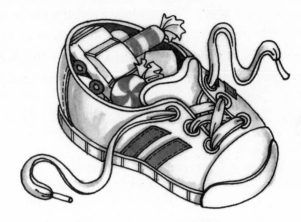

December 6 is a special day for children in Holland. They celebrate St. Nicholas' Day. Children leave their wooden shoes, stockings, or even modern shoes by the fireplace the evening of December 5. The next morning they find their shoes filled with pencils, trinkets, and candy! They pretend St. Nicholas, called *Sintecklaas*, has passed by the roof on his white horse! Later that day, the good bishop rides through town dressed in his robes and miter. Children tell stories of the good priest who lived hundreds of years ago and gave money and help to those in need.

One story tells of a poor father with three daughters. The oldest wanted to marry but had no dowry. Passing by the low window of their small room, Nicholas overheard her crying. After dark he returned and tossed some coins down the chimney. A few even fell into some stockings hanging there to dry! The old priest's eyes sparkled when he married the woman and her true love. Everyone wondered who had provided the dowry money.

Again, the second daughter needed dowry to marry. Once again the coins were found at the bottom of the chimney.

Finally, the third girl needed dowry, and this time the father discovered Bishop Nicholas passing the window. The father kept the mysterious giver's secret for many years. St. Nicholas is remembered as a loving, anonymous giver. That means no one knew where his gifts came from. That reminded the people who received gifts to give thanks to God.

*A **note for grown-ups**: Your child probably will be unfamiliar with the idea of a marriage dowry. A dowry was a gift of money or property or other goods that a young woman brought to her husband at their marriage. A woman without a dowry often found it impossible to find someone to marry. No dowry, no husband. This is still true in a few parts of the world today.*

Make a Christmas Memory

★ Put out your shoes on St. Nicholas' Eve like the Dutch children! Remember to give thanks to God for the goodies.

★ Read Matthew 6:3–4. Give your children extra chores so they can earn money to give anonymously to someone in need.

★ During the first week of December, our family enjoys the American Santa Claus myth, which originated with St. Nicholas' life. We take the children's picture with Santa Claus, make reindeer decorations, and do other secular crafts and Christmas activities until December 6. Then we put all the Santa decorations away so that the focus of Christmas is Jesus. We want our Christmas to be a holy day. We put gifts under the tree in piles sorted by giver rather than receiver to help us focus on giving for Jesus' birthday.

• •

Thank God for allowing us to know the witness of Christian saints like Bishop Nicholas.

 22

BIRD STUDY

Once a master teacher took her student to an aviary. They entered a large cage filled with twittering and flashes of color. Stepping out, they spied a direction sign to the finch cages. Inside one were goldfinches, waxbills, societies, and strawberry finches. The student even spotted a Lady Gould finch. "Watch their behavior closely," the teacher said.

After 10 minutes of watching, the teacher asked, "Which breed would Jesus be if He'd come to earth as a bird?"

Used to probing questions, the student thought a minute. "The strawberry finch has a beautiful song to praise God. The goldfinch delights God's eye. The society helps nest eggs from other birds, and the Lady Gould is like a rainbow promise."

The student watched a while longer. He noticed that like most bird societies, this one had a pecking order. The strawberry had to perch at least two inches from the goldfinch. Any closer and the goldfinch would screech and peck at the strawberry's feet. The Lady Gould could sit within an inch of the goldfinch before threatening challenges were issued. It seemed all the birds had fixed distances among themselves—all except the waxbill. Any bird could sit by it. The bird was obviously at the bottom of the pecking order. The student answered, "Jesus would be the waxbill there."

Smiling, the teacher said, "Explain."

What do you think the student said?

Make a Christmas Memory

★ Jesus could have come to earth like a mighty eagle or a glorious peacock, but He came like that little waxbill so that everyone could be near Him. Put the Baby Jesus piece from your créche onto various surfaces like a silk scarf, a piece of lace, and a velour robe. Discuss how people might have treated Baby Jesus if He lay on these. Then put the piece on straw. How did people really treat Jesus when He was born? Why did God, who could have chosen anything, pick the straw?

★ Set out treats for the birds like people do on Christmas in Norway. String Cheerios cereal, cranberries, popcorn, bacon rinds, apple pieces, or bits of bread or toast. Peanut-buttered pinecones are fun too. Spread peanut butter on pinecones, then role them in birdseed. Hang them in a tree by a window.

• •

Whistle a Christmas song to Jesus like the birds do!

LUKE 2 PARTY

Warmth flowed from the eager faces around the kitchen table. Oranges, candles, a roll of red ribbon, pins, and cellophane-tipped toothpicks littered the surface. Little John Mark squeezed in by the bowl of gumdrops mixed with mini-marsh-mallows and candies.

"First of all, we're glad everybody made it tonight!" Mr. Wendler said. John Mark looked over at Carlan's family. He'd invited them. Barbara reached for Paige's hand. Paige's family was her pick. The grown-ups looked at Mr. Wendler.

"We're going to make Kristingles first, and then practice some of the carols we'll sing as we go around the neighbor-hood later. Each of you grab an orange, and I'll explain."

Since the Wendler family made new Kristingles each year, the children knew how to help their friends. While each pinned on the ribbon and stuck in the candle, Mrs. Wendler explained that Kristingles are a Welsh tradition that reminds people that Jesus is the Light of the world. The orange represents the world; the candle represents Jesus come into the world. The red ribbon surrounds the world, and some families mark John 3:16 on it. The toothpicks pushed into the circumference stand for the red, yellow, black, and white races God created, whom He blesses with His good gifts, symbolized by the candies.

Later Barbara and Paige watched their flickering flames as the frosty air tugged them. Each time they knocked on a door and began singing, people came to listen. The carolers finished at each house singing, "We Wish You a Merry Christmas." When the last neighbor had been greeted, John Mark and Carlan raced home. They knew the hot cider and fresh donuts would come right after Dad read Luke 2 from the Bible.

John Mark's robe and a towel would make him a shepherd this year. Carlan had brought a sword so he could be the census-taker. The invitations always said children could dress up for a pantomime during the Bible reading if they liked.

Mrs. Wendler smiled at the backs of the little boys. She hugged Mr. Wendler. "The Luke 2 party is my favorite Christmas party," she said.

Make a Christmas Memory

★ Host a Luke 2 party at your house this year! Let each of your children write an invitation to one family. You can ask guests to bring cider while you furnish Kristingle supplies and donuts.

★ Join your church group's caroling ministry to people in nursing homes and hospitals. Consider taking along Christmas decorations to give away. This is an appropriate way to give charity food baskets without embarrassment.

• •

Sing "O Little Town of Bethlehem" and think of Jesus and Kristingles as you sing about the "everlasting Light."

UPSIDE-DOWN BIBLE STORY

Meggen watched as her teacher turned the big black Bible upside down on her lap. "Now that you've heard Luke 2 again, I'm going to see if I can fool you by telling the story with wrong pieces. If you hear me say something that's not really the way it was, raise your hand."

Meggen poised her right hand, ready to fire it up. "Here we go," the teacher said. "Once upon a time, in a magic kingdom, there lived a wicked king." Meggen's hand flew up. "Meggen," the teacher called.

"It wasn't a fairy tale. It really happened about 2,000 years ago."

"Okay, you caught me. So about 2,000 years ago, Caesar Augustus decided to tax everyone. He said that everyone had to go to their ancestral birthplace. This meant Joseph had to go to Bethlehem. Since Mary was about nine months pregnant, he left her home."

Hands shot up. Meggen giggled. "Joseph took Mary along," someone said.

"Caught me again." The teacher raised her eyebrows. "So then Mary and Joseph traveled to Bethlehem. Joseph had phoned in a motel reservation, so when they arrived, they had a nice room with a shower."

All the children were giggling now. "No! They didn't have phones!"

Or showers either, Meggen thought.

"All right, they didn't phone ahead, but the town had plenty of inns, so they tumbled wearily into a queen-size bed."

By now some children were laughing so hard, they were crying. "No queen-size bed?" the teacher asked.

"No beds!" came the chorus.

"So they arrived in Bethlehem, but there were no rooms. They made their way to a stable, and Mary started labor pains. Awhile later, Baby Jesus was born. Mary and Joseph wrapped Him in a blanket and laid Him in their suitcase."

Hands were waving everywhere. "In a manger!" several children called.

"Yes, in a manger," said the teacher. She smiled at the children as they calmed down, lowering her voice. "And it sounds like you know the story very well indeed!"

Make a Christmas Memory

★ Tell the part of the Luke 2 story about the shepherds. Then turn the Bible upside down and tell it with a lot of mistakes!

★ Make an ornament for your Sunday school teacher. Push a small object like a jingle bell into a balloon. Blow it up to ornament size. Soak yarn, braid, or rickrack in liquid starch and wind it around the balloon. Leave small spaces open like a lattice. Let dry two days. If desired, spray on snow or glue on glitter. Let dry. Pop the balloon and carefully pull it out. Add a hanger and a Christmas greeting!

No crisp sterile sheeting
Or Plexiglas tray,
No hospital clipboards
Where Christ Jesus lay;
But strong gentle fingers,
Some clean, freshened straw,
And patterns of wood grain
Were what Jesus saw.
Away in that manger,
No crib for a bed.
No bright rainbow bumper
Or mobile o'er head.
Still stars in the heavens
Shone on Him their lights,
Surrounding sweet Jesus
With marvelous sights.

CHRISTMAS CARDS

Although Christmas was started by God, Christmas cards began in England. During Victorian times, boarding school boys got heavy paper from the headmaster. They were expected to color a seasonal border around the edges. Although they regularly wrote home, this became a special Christmas letter. That idea developed into pre-inked letters and cards manufactured by printers.

Make a Christmas Memory

★ Make your own cards this year. Cut out simple Christmas shapes, like stars, bells, or angels, from old cards or sketch your own. Place the shapes on top of a piece of plain folded paper. Dip a toothbrush into liquid poster paint. Scrape the top of the bristles with a butter knife to spatter the paint onto the card. Try another color if you like. Let dry, then lift off the paper symbol. The space beneath it will be white. Outline that area if you wish. Write *Merry Christmas* in the white space and write a personal message or poem inside the card.

★ Write a family letter typed like a newspaper page, with each member contributing a story or a drawing. Be sure to include a family photo too. Photocopy your newspaper and send it every-where!

★ Make a Christmas card for Jesus. Chalk a picture on the sidewalk or put colored water in a squirt bottle and squirt the outline in the snow. You can make letters with rocks, twigs, or snowballs!

★ Make a pop-up card. Cut a strip of stiff paper 8″ × 2½″ inches. Fold it in half and then up on one side as illustrated in (a). Fold the other side to match (b). Unfolded, your paper would like (c). Fold a different sheet of stiff paper as your card. Glue one side of the strip inside as illustrated in (d). Spread glue on the other side of the strip (e). Close the card and let dry. On a separate piece of paper, draw a figure you like. Ours is a shepherd with his arms outstretched. Glue this to the middle of the open strip (f). Crease the fold through the body and carefully fold the figure down. When you open the card, the figure pops out, saying, "The Christ is born in Bethlehem!"

• • • • • • • • • • • • • • • • •

Save all the Christmas cards you receive. Place them in a basket. Beginning the day after Christmas, each family member can draw one out and pray for that sender during family devotions or prayer time.

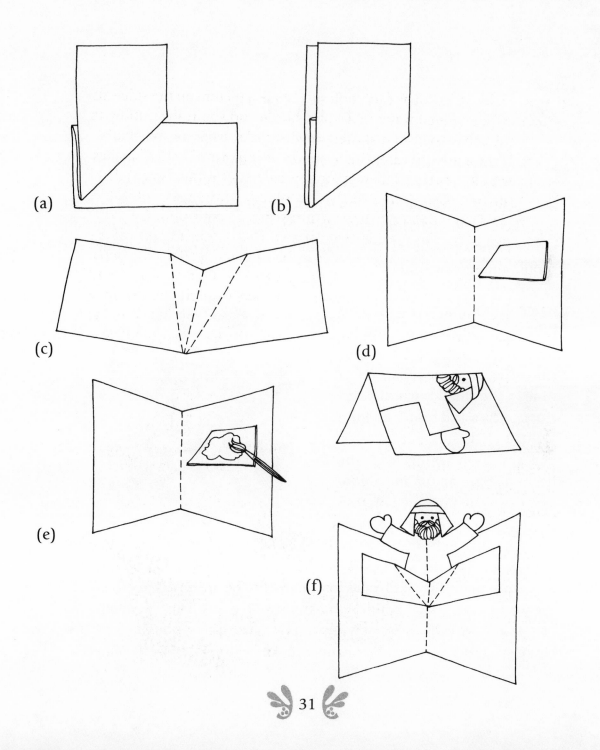

St. Francis

Did you ever pretend that late at night, your dolls and stuffed animals could talk? That idea came from someone born about 700 years ago in Italy. Before too long, this person landed in jail because of his wild carousing. There he thought long and hard and decided to become a Christian monk. Francis gave up all his wealth and spent the rest of his life living very simply and serving God.

Today, St. Francis is remembered all around the world for his love of all creatures and his idea to act out the Christmas story. This happened for the first time in the small town of Greccio. Francis asked his friend John Velitta to help him put on a live pageant. John arranged for the hay, a manger, an ox, and a donkey. Costumed people stood in place. Then Francis came with other monks and townspeople carrying candles and torches. The wonder of Bethlehem filled the night, and many people were deeply moved.

Since that time, Christmas pageants have been reenacted all around the world. Later, small Bethlehem figures were made that the Italians call *presepe* and we call *créches*. When you play with your créche or act in the church pageant, you might remember the man who loved God, Francis.

Make a Christmas Memory

★ Some time after Francis lived, the Irish Christians passed down the idea that, in honor of Christ's birth, the animals could talk for one hour at midnight on Christmas Eve. If they really could talk, what would they say to you?

★ Try another old tradition. Set a small manger or box on the table. Put a bit of straw nearby. Whenever someone serves another person during the Christmas season, he or she may put a straw in the manger to "soften Baby Jesus' bed." Place Jesus in the manger on Christmas Eve.

★ Bethlehem literally means "house of bread." In Germany, women make gingerbread houses at Christmastime. Roll out any gingerbread recipe and cut six identical squares. (Any size is okay.) Use four squares for the walls and two for the roof. First, glue the roof together like an A-frame. Use thick icing for your "glue." Let dry. Then ice the four walls together. Let dry. Prop the roof on top of the walls. Fill in the open triangles in the front and back with iced gumdrops or small candies. Let dry. Decorate the roof with cookies and candy. You might find out if anyone can guess what this house has to do with Bethlehem!

• •

Say St. Francis' prayer:

> Lord make me an instrument of Thy peace.
> Where there is hatred, let me sow love.
> Where there is injury, let me sow pardon.
> Where there is discord, let me sow union.
> Where there is doubt, let me sow faith.
> Where there is despair, let me sow hope.
> Where there is darkness, let me sow light.
> Where there is sadness, let me sow joy.

RIDDLES

From heav'n above to earth I come
To bring good news to ev'ryone!
Glad tidings of great joy I bring
To all the world and gladly sing:

To you this night is born a child
Of Mary, chosen virgin mild;
This newborn child of lowly birth
Shall be the joy of all the earth.

This is the Christ, God's Son most high,
Who hears your sad and bitter cry;

He will Himself your Savior be
And from all sin will set you free.

The blessing which the Father planned
The Son holds in His infant hand
That in His kingdom, bright and fair,
You may with us His glory share.

These are the signs which you will see
To let you know that it is He:
In manger bed, in swaddling clothes
The child who all the earth upholds.

© 1978 *Lutheran Book of Worship.* Used by permission.

Do you like "Who Am I" riddles? Let's try
some Christmas riddles:

I lived in Nazareth.
I worked with wood.
My father was Jacob.
Who am I?

I was rich and powerful.
I lived in Rome.
I decreed a census.
Who am I?

If you look at Luke 1 and 2 and Matthew 1 and 2, you'll find names such as *Zechariah, Gabriel, Elizabeth, John, Mary, Caesar Augustus, Quirinius,* lots of ancestors, the *Magi,* and *King Herod.* Make up some riddles of your own about these people.

Martin Luther, the Protestant reformer, made up a riddle song while rocking his little boy Han's crib one Christmas Eve. The song is printed on page 34. Sing the stanzas together and guess who is speaking.

Make a Christmas Memory

★ Play the guessing game a little differently. Think up a Christmas word such as *manger, stable, shepherd, myrrh,* or *census.* Then put objects that start with the letters of your word in a bag. For example, if you choose *manger:* put a **m**ap, **a**ngel, **n**ickel, **g**lue, **e**gg, and **r**uler in the bag. The team that gets this bag must guess the object's first letters and arrange them to spell a Christmas word—in this case, *manger.* You might want to tell your pastor about this game for a church family night.

★ Here's another guessing game. Pin a Christmas character's name to each family member's back. Who can figure out their hidden name by asking others yes-and-no questions about the character? (No fair guessing a name until the very end.)

★ How many of those names in Jesus' ancestry in Matthew 1 does your family recognize? Read about them in the Bible or a Bible storybook.

• •

Dress up in white sheets and garland halos. Pretend to be the angel singing "From Heaven Above."

SANTA LUCIA

The tray looked just right. Ansley had spent her own money at the bakery the day before. The buns were big and golden. She made instant coffee and set two steaming mugs next to the buns. Smoothing down her white nightgown, she reached for the wreath with the candles. She'd light the candles when Mom took a picture, but for now, it was safer to balance it on her head unlit!

Ansley stepped slowly up the stairs and nudged open her parents' bedroom door with her hip. Good, they're still asleep, she thought. She began to sing the old familiar song about Santa Lucia, a young girl who was killed way back in the second century because she was a Christian.

Mom woke up first, sat up in bed, and smiled. Then Dad pretended to be sleeping until Ansley set the tray near his nose. "What's this? Coffee in my dreams?" he muttered.

Ansley laughed and said, "Happy Santa Lucia Day, Daddy!"

Even though December 13 is one of the longest nights of the year in the northern part of Sweden, candles and love light up the morning!

Make a Christmas Memory

★ Make your own Saint Lucy buns.

2 pkgs. dry yeast

½ cup warm water

½ cup milk

saffron or yellow food coloring

½ cup sugar

1 tsp. salt

2 eggs, beaten

¼ cup butter, softened

5 cups flour (separated)

½ cup chopped raisins or citron

¼ cup chopped almonds

1 tbsp grated lemon peel

Dissolve yeast in water. Set aside. Scald milk. Cool. Add a pinch of crushed saffron or yellow food coloring, sugar, salt, eggs, butter, and 2½ cups flour. Beat until smooth. Add raisins or citron, almonds, lemon peel, and 2½ cups flour. Stir, then knead 10 minutes. Cover and let rise one hour. Punch down and shape into 8″ long strands. Curve each strand into an S shape and space them on greased baking sheets. Let rise one hour. Heat oven to 375° and bake 20 minutes (You could braid the dough into one wreath. After baking, put four candles in it and garnish it with icing and candied fruits. Wear it if you dare!)

★ Swedish boys hang paper stars on a stick with a thread. Wearing tall, cone-shaped hats covered with foil stars, they carol to family and friends on the afternoon of December 13. Try it!

★ Less elaborate but still fun—make green pancakes in a wreath shape for breakfast today. Serve with strawberry syrup.

• •

Memorize Isaiah 60:1 and 3:

Arise, shine for your light has come. … Nations will come to your light, and kings to the brightness of your dawn.

ELIZABETH AND ZECHARIAH

Monday. He left for Jerusalem calling, "Shalom, Elizabeth," and he comes back stumbling, with no voice. He uses his hands to tell me he's seen an angel, and we'll have a child. I think my poor old husband is becoming senile. It happens. But I will miss his sharp mind and all his Hebrew humor. Ah me.

Eight weeks later. We've settled into a routine. Zechariah pours over the scrolls even more than before. It is good for a priest to know the holy words. I putter around inside slowly since I'm old too. I've been feeling my age lately. My stomach isn't so good.

Six weeks later. It's so strange. I don't feel like eating, but I'm getting fatter. Zechariah says it's the baby. Foolish old fellow—a baby. That's about as impossible as seeing an angel!

Four weeks later. There are strange flutterings in me. I dare not hope the impossible. How could I be pregnant? Nothing like this has happened in a thousand years—since Abraham and Sarah! Who are we that God would bless us?

Four weeks later. I stay inside, but my spirit soars. Songs just burst from my heart. The angel said, "A son." The angel said, "John!" I sway side to side, rocking my John in my womb! Oh, you blessed boy! Blessed *Adonai!* The Lord has done this for me! Bless the Lord! Oh, bless the Lord!

Six weeks later. Another miracle in the family! Cousin Mary came today. I threw open my arms in greeting, and John leaped in greeting too. Then I knew. Mary is with child, with the Holy Child. She will bear the Messiah! What wonders are these? Zechariah looks on with silent joy. He shows Mary the prophesies. Oh, to live in such days!

Make a Christmas Memory

★ Read the whole story of Elizabeth and Zechariah in Luke 1. Sing the Magnificat or Nunc Dimitis from your hymnal. If you are using the yarn ball idea from pages 13–14, wrap the following in reverse order on the outside of the ball, making it bigger. It will then have 25 objects inside, one for each day of December until Christmas. Or use these ideas for devotions during the 12 days of Christmas, singing the songs as well.

Verses 5–7: *A flat stone.* The Ten Commandments were written on stone. How many of them can you name right now?

Verses 8–10: *Perfume.* The sense of smell is one of our strongest senses. How might a smell like incense help a worshiper?

Verses 11–17: *Card that says, "Prediction."* What would this as yet unborn person do? Does God have predictions for us too? (See Jeremiah 29:11.)

Verses 18–22: *A whistle.* Why would Zechariah find a whistle useful now?

Verses 23–25: *Picture of an older woman.* What do you think Elizabeth's neighbors said when they saw her six months pregnant?

Verses 26–29: *Paper angel.* What angels can you name?

Verses 30–33: *An unequal sign (≠).* How was the prediction about Jesus different from the prediction about John?

Verses 34–38: *White cloth.* What does *holy* mean? Look it up in a dictionary.

Verses 39–45: *Blindfold.* Faith is believing without seeing. Who believed without seeing in verse 45?

Verses 57–66: *Chalk.* Act out this scene for fun!

● ●

Say Gabriel's words to each other: Nothing is impossible with God.

CHRISTMAS TREES

When the 13 colonies fought England to become the United States of America, the Christmas tree tradition came to America. It's true! The English hired German soldiers to fight on their side. In Germany, there was already a tradition of cutting an evergreen tree and putting lit candles on it at Christmas.

During the Middle Ages, church groups put on plays about creation and the first sins of Adam and Eve. The props included a fir tree hung with apples. That's why you often see apple ornaments. Still later, Communion wafers were put on the tree to remind us of Jesus' gift of salvation to the world. These wafers were sometimes cut into Christian symbols called *chrysmons.* Now, all kinds of ornaments are sold. You might look at your collection to see which ones most help you think about Jesus and the beauty of God's Christmas Gift!

Make a Christmas Memory

★ Look for a German springerle rolling pin. These pins roll small symbols into cookie dough. The square cookies can be hung on the tree.

★ People in Denmark celebrate "Cut-and-Paste Day" in December. Families make fabric and paper ornaments, often using red and white, their national colors. Here are two you might make.

Enlarge Pattern A on page 43. Trace and cut it from heavy red or white paper. Fold the shape into a cone and glue the tab inside. Add a paper handle and fill with nuts or red hots.

Cut six 3″ circles from heavy foil. Fold the six circles in half and cut as indicated in illustration (B). Cut a 3″ circle from cardboard and cover it completely with foil. Slip the six folded foil circles vertically onto the horizontal cardboard foil circle as shown in illustration (C). Spread the folds open so edges touch for a three-dimensional star! String and hang.

★ Celebrate Christmas with Martin Luther. Stand outside holding candles tonight and sing, "From Heaven Above to Earth I Come."

• •

Think about all the ways God has given the world light—sun, moon, stars, lightning bugs, neon fish, certain chemicals, lasers. Praise Him for all of these, including the best Light (see John 8:12).

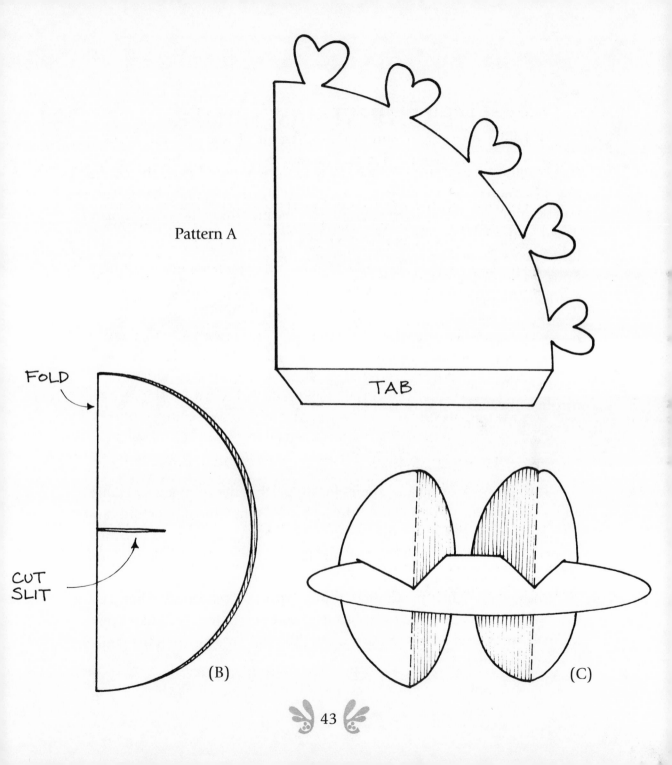

Pattern A

TAB

FOLD

CUT
SLIT

(B)

(C)

THE CHRISTMAS SPIDER

Long, long ago, a poor Russian woman wondered how she could make Christmas special for her two children. Times were very hard. Papa had been snatched away by enemy soldiers five months earlier. The woman gazed at the falling snow. How can I celebrate Jesus' birth? There'll be no cookies, bright ribbons, paper ornaments, or presents this year. She thought harder. At least I could cut a Christmas tree from the woods, she told herself.

The children helped their mother pull a little fir tree through the snow and into their cottage. It stood bravely in a corner, looking a bit forlorn, but spreading its wintergreen smell through the tiny room.

The family ate bread and apples for supper, but the youngest saved his apple, polished it, and hung it on the little tree. When the older child saw this, she pulled her only ribbon from her hair and tied it to another branch. The three stared at the tree awhile and then walked to midnight mass at the village church.

They greeted their neighbors, calling *"Hristos Razdajetsja!"* They saw that many other fathers and older brothers were absent too. Fervent prayers for their safety were added to the more traditional prayers. Then the families walked home.

The mother tucked her two sleepy children into their bed, then she knelt to pray. Tears trickled down her cheeks as she recalled other Christmases. Unknown to her, a small spider had silently watched and listened all evening long. When the mother's eyes finally closed, the little spider went to work.

The next morning, as sunlight glinted through the windowpanes, the mother gasped. "Children, children! Come and see!" She wrapped her arms around them as they stood gaping at the miracle. Crisscrossing lines of silvery web covered the tree from top to bottom!

"Mother, this is the most beautiful tree in the village! If only Papa could see." Just then the door opened, and Papa stumbled in, weary but overjoyed to be home.

That night the candle stubs gently lighted the tree's spidery beauty. The mother looked from the tree to the glowing eyes of her family. "Thank You, God, for Your gift of Jesus, for Your gift of family, and for Your gift of a spider."

Make a Christmas Memory

★ If you've ever wondered why silvery strands of tinsel hang on Christmas trees, now you know the legend! Make a giant web by running yarn or string all over a room or two. Ask your children to unravel it. For example, run one string under a sofa leg to a dining room chair, to the edge of a shelf, back under the edge of the rug, and end around a doorknob. Run a second string over and under the first, as well as winding it around separate objects. Make the web as simple or as complex as you like. At the end of each string, put a note describing a prize—a bowl of ice cream or popcorn, a horsyback ride to bed, a serenade from Dad, an indoor picnic, etc.

★ Winding in and out of places is fun. Try a one-house progressive dinner—appetizer in the bedroom, salad in the den, main course in the kitchen, and dessert in the bathroom! Guests must work for their supper by singing a Christmas song before each course is served!

Bugs

I tread on sidewalk highways—stop.
Minute metallic rush hours—look.
A-hum with scurried buzzes—listen.
Proceed with caution!

How intricate God must be—stop.
To make such tiny traffic—look.
I marvel at His detail—listen.
Proceed with attention!

WRAPPING PAPER

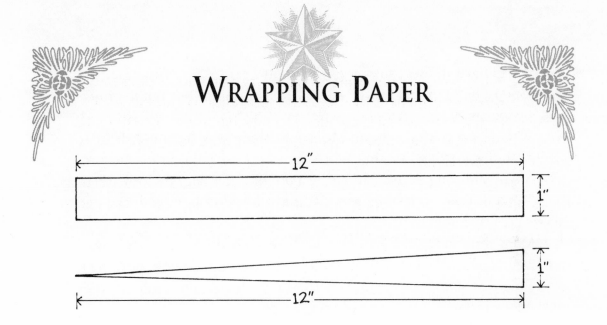

These are too pretty to toss out, Mom thought as she looked at the Christmas paper scraps left after wrapping gifts.

"Mommy, what can I give my teacher this year?" Sarah asked as she came into the dining room.

Mom looked at Sarah and then at the scraps. "Go call your brother," she said. "I think we'll manage very well!"

Josh and Sarah used their rulers to measure 1" × 12" strips of wrapping paper. "These will roll up into tube-shaped beads," Mom explained. "If you want other shapes, try a triangle—just make it 12" long. Or cut a 12" × ½" triangle for a shorter bead."

When they had drawn their shapes, the children cut them out. Then they rolled each one tightly around a nail. "Put one dot of glue on the last bit of each roll-up to keep it stuck," Mom said. "They need to dry now, so we'll finish them tomorrow."

"Can I have all these snippings to put on a card?" Sarah asked.

"Sure! Put them in a bowl," Mom said as she and Josh put the rulers and scissors away.

The next day after school, Mom had some wax from old dripless white candles melting in a tin can. (*Note:* Don't use paraffin for this project.) "Why did you put that can inside a pot of water, Mom?" Josh asked.

"It's a double boiler this way. I want to be sure the wax doesn't go above 212° and smoke."

Mom showed the children how to dip each nail into the candle wax, remove it, count slowly to 10, and dip it a second time before pushing it into a piece of Styrofoam to dry. When they had filled the Styrofoam, they pushed the last nails into some of Sarah's clay.

When every bead was finished, Josh and Sarah cleared the newspapers from the floor and countertop while Mom cleaned up the stove.

"How long will the beads take to dry?" Josh asked.

"Let's give them until tomorrow," Mom said.

"Are we going to the dentist?" Sarah asked the next day when Mom handed her a piece of dental floss.

"No, silly!" Josh answered. "The floss is for stringing the beads, right Mom?"

"Right!"

Josh and Sarah spent the next hour laying the beads in colorful patterns and then stringing them. Mom was the guinea pig to be sure the necklaces would fit over an adult's head. Finally each precious necklace was put in a box and gift-wrapped.

"We have scraps again!" Mom laughed.

Make a Christmas Memory

It's a lot more work for children to make gifts, but if you limit the number, they can learn the joy of giving of one's self. Here are some other ideas for handmade gifts.

★ Make jam, cookies, or candy together, or let your child select them at the store. Arrange the treats on a child-decorated paper plate or basket.

★ Put cloves, cinnamon sticks, grated nutmeg, and allspice into cheesecloth squares. Tie with fabric strips. Pack with a box of tea! You can pack basil, marjoram, thyme, and rosemary with olive oil and tomato sauce for an Italian twist.

★ Clay is great for young friends. Mix 2 cups flour with 1 cup salt and 4 teaspoons cream of tartar. Add 1 cup boiling water and 2 tablespoons oil. Knead. Tint the clay with food coloring.

★ Make a tree ornament from a wooden curtain ring (from the hardware store). Glue moss or small dried flowers to the bottom. Add a tiny crèche from a craft store or an angel cut from a Christmas card. Add a hanger.

★ Trace your child's hand onto a plain potholder. Stitch around the outline with colored cord and add a message.

• •

Jot the names of people you are giving Christmas gifts to onto the squares of your June calendar. When June comes, give each person their second present by asking God to bless one person each day.

ECHO PANTOMIME

The leader reads each line while doing the actions. The family copies or "echoes" the leader.

Clop, clop.
  Step in place.
Clop, clop.
  Step in place.
Donkey feet plod the road.
  Slap thighs.
Stop, stop.
  Put one hand up in halt motion.
Stop, stop.
  Put other hand up in halt motion.
So far to go to Bethlehem.
  Shade eyes and peer ahead.

Clop, clop.
  Step in place.
Clop, clop.
  Step in place.
Donkey feet plod the road.
  Slap thighs.
Joseph walks s-l-o-w-ly
  Step slowly.
Mary is so-o-o-o-o
  Bend head upwards.
Tired.
  Drop head down.

Clop, clop.
Step in place.
Clop, clop.
Step in place.
Donkey feet plod the road.
Slap thighs.
Stop, stop.
Put one hand up in halt motion.
Stop, stop.
Put other hand up in halt motion.
Here we are in Bethlehem!
Look around.
Ahhhhhhhhh!
Smile.

Knock, knock.
Knock one fist into other open palm.
Knock, knock.
Knock again.
Tired knuckles rap the door.
Knock slowly.
No room!
Pretend to open door.
No room?
Shake head sadly.
Joseph feels l-o-w.
Hang head.
Mary is so-o-o-o-o
Bend head upwards.
Tired.
Drop head down.

Clop, clop.
Step in place.
Clop, clop.
Step in place.
Donkey feet plod the road.
Slap thighs.
Stop, stop.
Put one hand up in halt motion.
Stop, stop.
Put other hand up in halt motion.
A stable for the night—
Make an A-frame with fingertips.
Hmmmmmmmmm.
Sigh.

Soon, soon,
Put palms up to cheeks—oh no!
Soon, soon,
Repeat.
A newborn cries!
Rock arms.
Angels shout!
Throw up both arms!
Shepherds seek!
Shade eyes.
Joseph bows l-o-w.
Bow head.
And Mary is so-o-o-o-o
Bend head upward.
Glad!
Drop head and smile!

Make a Christmas Memory

★ Many Christian bookstores sell flannelgraph packets of the Nativity story. Punch out the paper objects and let the children tell the Christmas story as they lay the figures on a square yard of blue felt. Copy the figures on this page if you wish.

★ Make fingerpuppets from toilet paper rolls or cut up wrapping paper tubes as shown. Make a donkey, Mary, Joseph, Baby Jesus, innkeeper, and shepherds. Use the echo pantomime as a play script. You can even make a portable stage using two tension rods draped with dish towels in a doorframe.

Jesus came as a baby just like us!
Thank God for Baby Jesus and any
other babies that you know.

ANGEL QUIZ

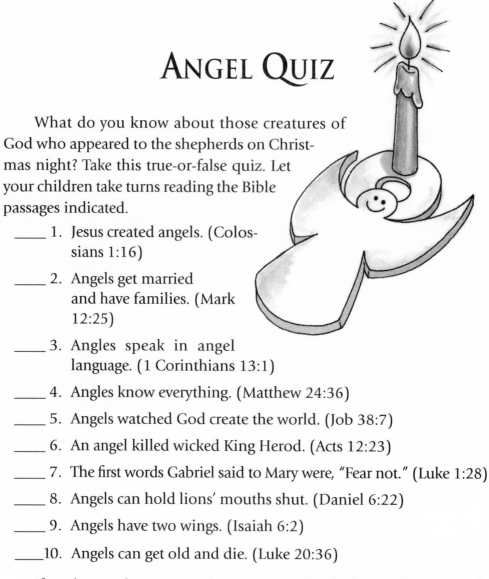

What do you know about those creatures of God who appeared to the shepherds on Christmas night? Take this true-or-false quiz. Let your children take turns reading the Bible passages indicated.

_____ 1. Jesus created angels. (Colossians 1:16)

_____ 2. Angels get married and have families. (Mark 12:25)

_____ 3. Angles speak in angel language. (1 Corinthians 13:1)

_____ 4. Angles know everything. (Matthew 24:36)

_____ 5. Angels watched God create the world. (Job 38:7)

_____ 6. An angel killed wicked King Herod. (Acts 12:23)

_____ 7. The first words Gabriel said to Mary were, "Fear not." (Luke 1:28)

_____ 8. Angels can hold lions' mouths shut. (Daniel 6:22)

_____ 9. Angels have two wings. (Isaiah 6:2)

_____10. Angels can get old and die. (Luke 20:36)

If you've ever been amazed to see a new kind of caterpillar, butterfly, or bird, imagine the thrill of seeing angels! There will be so much to learn!

Make a Christmas Memory

★ Roll clay into a half-inch thick slab. Trace the angel or photocopy it. Use the pattern to trace two angels in the clay. Cut them out. Push a candle into the shaded circle to make a depression. Let dry. Paint and let dry. Use your angel candleholders for a candle-light supper one night during the 12 days of Christmas. Place the manger piece from your créche set between the candles.

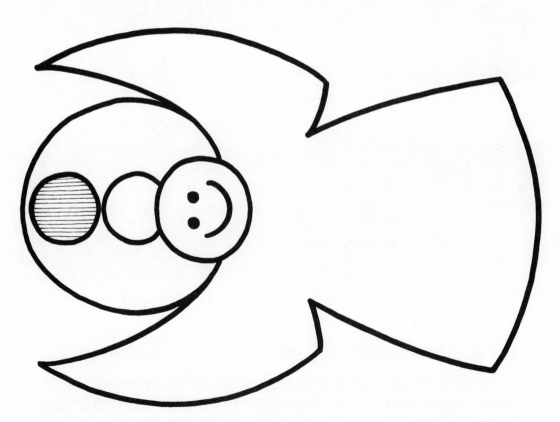

★ Make angel puppets from stiff paper glued to a wooden clothespin or cardboard tube. Pull the strings to make the wings flap. See illustration.

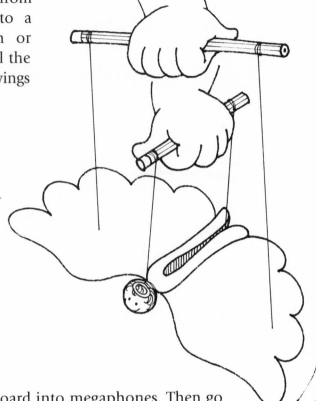

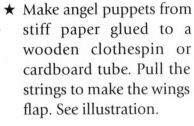

★ Roll pieces of cardboard into megaphones. Then go outside and sing "Joy to the World" through them. Try long-distance caroling to grandparents and friends over the phone!

★ Take a look at what angels say when they talk to God. Read Isaiah 6:3; Luke 2:14; Revelation 5:12; and Revelation 7:12. How does angel talk compare to human talk?

....

Sing "All Night, All Day." The words and music are on the next page.

56

ALL NIGHT, ALL DAY

Spiritual

Spiritual

1. Day is dy-in' in the west; an-gels watch-in' o-ver me, my Lord.
2. Now I lay me down to sleep; an-gels watch-in' o-ver me, my Lord.
3. Thy love stay with me through the night; an-gels watch-in' o-ver me, my Lord. And

Sleep, my child, and take your rest; an-gels watch-in' o-ver me.
Pray the Lord my soul to keep; an-gels watch-in' o-ver me.
wake me with the morn-ing light; an-gels watch-in' o-ver me.

Refrain

All night, all day, an-gels watch-in' o-ver me, my Lord.

All night, all day, an-gels watch-in' o-ver me.

THE CENSUS-TAKER

The wind whipped the soldier's red cape next to the census-taker's head. He scowled at the man, but the Roman soldier stared straight ahead, back erect, lance held stiffly to the side. Marcus turned to see the line of scraggly people in front of his table. Why anyone would want to know how many of these miserable people live in this flea-bitten country is beyond me, he thought. If Caesar expects to get tax money from these tattered ragbags, he might as well expect to squeeze water from a stone!

Marcus studied the man making his family's sign in the clay tablet. Men like this are only fit for cleanup duty in Rome's army! Look at this one! He's probably never read anything in his miserable life—no Socrates, no Vergil. What worthwhile thought ever entered his head? Marcus stared at the man's hands. Strong hands though, this one could pitch tents maybe. Still, give me a Greek slave any day over these religious fanatics.

Behind the man was a young woman with a baby folded into her waist-band. Thank the gods I have a cultured wife! Marcus thought. This one smells of a stable. My Julia is all fine oils and spices. She raises my son with discipline and loyalty to Rome. What kind of brat will this one raise—another insignificant Jew.

"Hurry up!" Marcus growled. The man stopped signing and looked into Marcus' eyes. Marcus shifted in his chair. "Move along," he barked. The man looked toward his wife and gently laid his arm on her waist. As they walked away, Marcus ground his teeth. What stupid people! That man acted as if he and I were equals! What a fool! No one worth anything will ever come out of this dusty little Jewish village.

"Next!" Marcus called. "Sign under this name!" He pointed to where the register read, *Joseph, Mary, Jesus.*

Make a Christmas Memory

★ That one Jewish baby made a great deal of difference to the world! He still does! As a family, remember foreign missions by choosing a specific mission that you could pray for regularly. Find ways for the children to earn money or make useful gifts to help spread the Good News that Jesus is our Savior. Write to Mission Education, 1333 S. Kirkwood Road, St. Louis, MO 63122-7295 for ideas.

★ Spread shaving cream on a cookie sheet and let young children illustrate this story in it. Pudding also works, and you get to lick it off too!

★ Make up a Christmas package with stickers, hard candies, Christmas decorations, colored ribbons, drawings from the children, etc., for a young person from your church who is attending college away from home. Be sure to include your children's retelling of the Christmas story, either a handwritten note or one dictated to you.

• •

Who are the Gentiles in Luke 2:32? Copy the words and tape them to the manger in your créche set. Read the words together.

COUPONS

"What are these envelopes taped all over my bedroom door?" Matt yelled. He was standing in front of his room, still holding his bookbag.

"I'm in the kitchen, Matt," Dad called.

Matt stared at the white envelopes and began reaching for one when he heard, "Don't open any!" from the kitchen. He dropped his bookbag and headed for the voice.

"How come you're home today?" Matt asked, reaching for an apple from the basket on the counter.

"It's just slow at work right now," Dad explained, "so the boss sent us home early."

Matt knew his parents had been talking quietly the last few evenings and stopped when he or his sister, Lara, got near. Lots of dads at school were laid off, and some of the kids talked about no presents for Christmas. So far Matt only had a few gifts under the tree from relatives. Did all the envelopes have something to do with this?

"So what's in the envelopes, Dad?"

"Presents, Matt!"

"Money?"

"No," Dad laughed. "But lots of good things don't cost money."

"So what's in them?"

Dad playfully wrestled Matt into an armlock. "Since when have you ever found out your presents before Christmas?"

Matt tickled Dad, and pretty soon the "Gaboozal Tickle Match" was on, with both of them rolling on the rug. They were having so much fun they didn't see Lara come in with white envelopes in her hand. "What are these?" she asked loudly.

Dad and Matt looked up. "Go put those back on your door!" Dad said.

"Maybe there's a 'Gaboozal Tickle Match' in one of them for a Christmas present," laughed Matt.

"Oooo—what a good idea," said Dad as he wiggled his fingers into Matt's unprotected side.

Make a Christmas Memory

★ Coupons for special activities make terrific gifts. You might date them by the month. Here are some ideas.

1. "High tea" served with all the company dishes when your child arrives home from school.

2. A Hugs-and-Kisses Day. Remember to blow kisses to God, too, and share some Hershey's chocolate kisses.

3. Plan an Assembly-Line Pizza Party for supper. Place English muffins, tomato sauce, cheese, etc., at separate stations.

4. Announce a Mystery Night and don't tell the children where they're going. You might have a candlelight picnic for dinner, play a flashlight I Spy game in the yard, or plan a supper exchange with a neighbor— you go to a friend's supper table and they go to yours.

5. Invite friends for a Paintbrush Cookie Fest. Use school paint box size brushes to paint colored icing on sugar cookies.

6. Hold a family Table Game Tournament with four or five games. Set up all the games and allow seven minutes to play each game. Keep points for first and second place at each game and treat winners to a mini-marshmallow toss—either they toss into losers' mouths or vice versa.

7. Announce a Guestroom Night and give the kids your room for an evening.

8. Prepare a Super Bag Lunch Special. Monogram everything. Use a marker to write "Favorite 4th-grader at our house" on a banana. Squirt "Star" on a sandwich with cheese. Print a note on a napkin. Add a rose with a gift tag and a heart-shaped piece of cake. Get creative!

9. Make a Free Dishwash Whenever Presented ticket. Make a ticket for any normal chore your child is assigned.

Consider using some of the other crafts and games from this book too!

• •

Many gifts come swathed
In paper,
A work of art.
The best gifts come sheathed
In skin,
A work of the heart.

BETHLEHEM

The history of Bethlehem in the Bible is marked by the stories of three mothers. The very first was the beautiful Rachel, favored wife of Jacob. All her adventures are told in Genesis chapters 29–35. She died in childbirth after naming her son Ben Oni, "child of my sorrows." Rachel was buried near Bethlehem, something people of Jesus' day still remembered. Read Matthew 2:17–18.

The second story tells of the foreigner Ruth, who returned to Bethlehem with her mother-in-law, Naomi. She announced her intention to believe in Naomi's God, and eventually Ruth married a wealthy man of the village. She bore a son, Obed, "servant of the Lord." Her life is described in the Old Testament book called Ruth. You will also find her name listed in Matthew 1:5 as one of the ancestors of Jesus. Her name listed there reminds us that Jesus came to be the Savior of all people, no matter their background or where they are from.

The third story is about the most familiar mother, Mary. She gives her Son the name Gabriel instructed, Jesus, "the Lord saves." It was in Bethlehem that Mary heard the words of the angels from local shepherds. After their story was spread, many visitors might have come to see Jesus. Eastern star-studiers—our Wise Men—followed the star God placed in the sky to Bethlehem, bringing gifts to the young Jesus. Many of the events Mary "pondered in her heart" happened in Bethlehem.

Three well-known Bible women all in the same town—God tucks mysteries everywhere.

Make a Christmas Memory

★ Draw a scene of Bethlehem on paper. Cut around three sides of trees and buildings, as illustrated, so they can be folded to stand up. You might draw your scene to the scale of your créche set and place the figures in your village scene.

★ Read Micah 5:2. Why do you think God chose one of the small cities of Judah as the birthplace for His Son?

★ Play a Bible fact game with dice. Set a family point goal and see if you can meet it. Roll the die. If a 1 is rolled, the player must name a man in the Bible. (Joseph, for example). If a 2 is rolled, name a woman in the Bible; 3, a place in the Bible; 4, an object mentioned in the Bible; 5, a book of the Bible; 6, say a Bible verse. Go round robin and give a point for each answer, but remember, no one can repeat what has already been said.

• •

Thank God for letting us exist in families with relationships that are lifelong. A great many of His creatures do not have enduring relationships.

ROOM FOR HIM

Is there room in your ♥ for Jesus?

Jeff was a big boy, but he had a problem learning. Knowing that Jeff had a disability and often forgot things, his loving Sunday school teacher searched the parts in the Christmas story for something important so he'd feel needed but not too challenged. The innkeeper! she thought. He has only two words to say, "No room."

Rehearsal went well Christmas Eve afternoon, and the teacher hurried home with her last-minute lists. Everything looked ready for a fairly polished performance.

That night under the lights, something better than "polished" happened. Jeff stood inside a cardboard door and peeked out to watch Joseph and Mary cross the stage. As they drew closer to his inn, he noticed how tired they seemed to be.

Knock, knock. The sound came on cue. "Do you have room for my wife and me?" Joseph called.

Jeff's eyes were misty as he stared at Joseph. After an awkward pause, the audience heard, "No room! No room!" whispered loudly from backstage.

In a bit of a daze, Jeff mumbled, "No room," into Joseph's weary face. But just as Joseph turned away, the big boy stepped out of his door and called, "But you can have my room!"

At first the audience chuckled, but then some began to get misty-eyed. They realized that Jeff's compassion was a small picture of God's love shared at Christmas.

Make a Christmas Memory

★ Play "What If" with Luke 2 by asking questions such as these: What if Joseph had refused to marry Mary? What if there had been no tax decree? What if there had been room at the inn? What if the shepherds thought they'd all seen something they'd better keep quiet about, so no one would think they were crazy? What if the angels had appeared to worshipers in the temple instead of shepherds? What if Jesus were born in Bethlehem today? Thank God for planning our salvation just right!

★ Make red doorhangers as illustrated. Write: Is there room in your ♥ for Jesus? Write the place and time of your Christmas worship service on the back of the doorhanger. Hang these in the neighborhood near your church and around your home.

★ Jeff was willing to give his own room for Jesus. What can you give Jesus for His birthday this year? What about a poem you've made up? A song you sing to Him all by yourself? A flower you grew, or bought, that you set on the altar? An ornament to hang on the church or family tree that you made for Him? (Jesus knows that serving others is a gift to Him, but young children often need to give a gift directly to Jesus.)

• •

Set a plate for Jesus one day as you begin a meal. Pray "Come Lord Jesus, be our guest; let Thy gifts to us be blessed." Reflect afterwards together on what Jesus thought of eating with you that day.

66

WINDOW LIGHTS

In Ireland, families place candles in their windows on Christmas Eve. A thick candle as big as two feet tall is set in the main window. Then either the youngest child or a child named Mary is given the honor of lighting this big candle. All other candles in the windows of the house are lit from this central one. Tradition says that these lights shine the way for any family, like Mary and Joseph, who needs shelter. Years ago, it was also a signal to any passing priests that they were welcomed in that house.

In many Irish towns, close to midnight, families gather at the highest place and look out at all the candles twinkling in the town. Families in our country often do the same as they drive around looking at Christmas lights, not only in windows but decorating the outsides of homes too. A midnight church service with hand-held candles also thrills Christians with the visible reminder of Jesus Christ, the Light of the world.

Make a Christmas Memory

★ Put candles in your windows on Christmas Eve too. Or use flashlights with a square of red cellophane banded to the top. Some people like to line their walkways with luminaries—candles placed inside paper bags half-full of sand.

★ What do you see out of each window in your home that can remind you of God's Christmas gift? Go look. Even a wall can recall how Jesus broke the wall sin put up between us and God.

★ Go outside in the evening when house lights are on. Look in your windows. What do you think people might see in your home that helps them know you love Jesus? Hold candles or flashlights.

★ Set your créche set outside on the ground. *You* be twinkling lights in the heavens, shining over Bethlehem that Christmas Eve long ago. The Bible says the stars "sang together" at creation (Job 38:7). Imagine their "song" at Jesus' birth! Sing star songs like "O Little Town of Bethlehem," "Joy to the World," and "Away in a Manger."

• •

Join Irish Christians in their traditional candle-lighting poem:

On Christmas Eve a candle light
To shine abroad through Christmas night,
That those who pass may see its glow
And walk with Christ a mile or so.

CHRISTMAS

This wasn't a surprise because he'd invited them every year. Like always, the kids started getting excited several weeks ahead. They knew the party would be fabulous. There'd be tables full of scrumptious food, great games, new videos, and best of all—expensive party favors.

On the party day, all the young guests arrived dressed in their party best. The door opened to a living room all decorated in red—shiny red bows, red birthday candles of all sizes, even the candies were red. After a quick "Happy birthday" to the host, most of the boys and girls dashed to the party-favor table, where toys and treats were piled high. Gifts were grabbed as they searched for the labels bearing their own names. Two boys pulled on the same large package.

"I had it first! Just let me see if it's for me!"

"No! I know it's mine. I'm sure it's the megaloputic numbwranger I told him I'd like."

Next to them were three girls trying to count how many favors each received.

"I think you have more than me. That's not fair," griped one.

A few of the other guests were stuffing goodies from the table into their mouths. This was one time no one said, "Don't eat too much," so they slathered jelly on crisp white rolls and cut out big hunks of pie.

A couple of boys were running around, shrieking and laughing, knocking over several of the fragile decorations. The birthday boy stood by the door, greeting the last of the arriving guests.

One of these last guests stood silently beside the door, surveying the wild scene. There were children ripping through wrapping paper, groaning over too-full tummies, and staring at video monitors. In the middle of the uproar stood the birthday boy, looking alone and forgotten.

The newcomer quietly slipped to the boy's side. "This is for you," he whispered in the boy's ear.

"A present for *me!*" the boy said, surprised.

"It is *your* birthday," came the answer.

The two sat down together and enjoyed the suspense of unwrapping the gift. Holding it carefully, the birthday boy beamed. "You did this yourself! It's just what I wanted!" They looked at each other like fast friends.

"Happy birthday and many more!" the quiet guest said. "Thanks so much!"

Make a Christmas Memory

★ Today is Jesus' birthday. Which of the guests at His party are you?

★ Put a "Happy Birthday, Jesus" on each Christian picture and object in your house.

★ Let children make place mats while adults are busy in the kitchen. Have them draw stable scenes—or a picture of their Christmas service—on paper with crayons or markers. Suggest that they write a birthday greeting to Jesus on it too. Cover with clear adhesive paper. Save these place mats in your memory scrapbook or box of Christmas decorations.

★ Cupholders add to the birthday celebration. Adapt the template on the next page to fit your cups and let the children color them with markers. Angels, shepherds, or singing people work well.

★ If you have a candle tree with twirling wooden slats on top, or a metal one with angels flying around tinkling bells, light it today and each day during the 12 days of Christmas. We like to have each family member select a Christmas song to sing. Our family of five sings five songs each of the 12 evenings. It's a great way to memorize carols.

Let us all with gladsome voice
Praise the God of heaven,
Who, to make our hearts rejoice,
His own Son has given.

Christ, our Lord and Savior dear,
Oh, be ever near us.
Be our joy throughout each
year.
Amen, Jesus, hear us.

Trace or photocopy and adapt to fit your cups.

glue

fold
down
for halo

THE TWELVE DAYS
OF CHRISTMAS

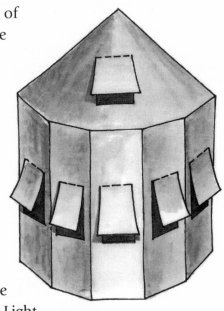

Elizabeth's dad put the 12 days of Christmas tower on the supper table Christmas Day. It was especially important to both of them because Mommy was now with Jesus in heaven.

"Okay, 'Lizbeth, open a door," Dad said.

Elizabeth picked one from the side. She liked to open one of the two top doors on Christmas Day and the other on Epiphany, the twelfth day. "Isaiah 49:6," she read.

Dad flipped through the Bible and then read, "I will also make You a Light for the Gentiles, that You may bring My salvation to the ends of the earth."

"That's one of my favorite names for Jesus: Light for the Gentiles. I'm a Gentile!" Elizabeth began writing the title with her calligraphy marker on a sheet of red paper. Other Chinese children, who weren't Christian like Elizabeth, would set out offerings by the pictures of parents or relatives who had died. Elizabeth liked to put this red paper full of names for Jesus next to her mother's picture. It reminded her that all of them would be together in heaven, praising Jesus with these words someday.

"Light for the Gentiles—Isaiah 49:6—there," Elizabeth said when she finished. "Right under Savior—Titus 2:13."

"Think we can get both 'Savior' and 'Light of the Gentiles' into our prayer?" Dad asked.

Elizabeth grinned. "We got all 12 in last year, Dad. I think two is going to be easy!"

They held hands and bowed their heads. "O Jesus, Savior," Elizabeth prayed, "we thank You so much for saving Mommy and all the others that keep You company in heaven. We praise You for being so loving that You are the Light for the Gentiles. Your kingdom is full of people of all races and colors. Please give Mom a kiss from us, and help our vacation time together to be fun. In Your name we pray. Amen."

Make a Christmas Memory

★ You can make a 12 days of Christmas tower by folding a piece of tagboard as indicated by the illustration. Fold a small piece of tagboard over the top for a roof. Attach fold-up doors with one of the following Bible texts under each one.

Isaiah 9:6 (Wonderful Counselor)

Isaiah 49:6 (Light for the Gentiles)

Matthew 1:23 (Immanuel)

Luke 2:11 (Christ the Lord)

John 1:29 (Lamb of God)

John 10:11 (Good Shepherd)

Acts 3:14 (Holy and Righteous One)

Romans 9:5 (God over All)

Romans 15:12 (Root of Jesse)

2 Thessalonians 3:16 (Lord of Peace)

Titus 2:13 (Savior)

Revelation 17:14 (Lord of Lords and King of Kings)

You can change the doors each year. Other passages to use include Haggai 2:7; Matthew 9:15; Matthew 11:19; Mark 1:24; John 1:41; John 1:49; John 6:48; John 6:51; John 10:7; John 11:25; John 14:6; Acts 10:42; Ephesians 2:20; Ephesians 5:23; Hebrews 2:10; Hebrews 4:14; 1 Peter 2:6; 2 Peter 1:19; and Revelation 22:16.

★ December 26 is traditionally Boxing Day in England. On this day, gift boxes, usually of food, are given to the elderly, sick, and clerks who serve the family. Share Christmas goodies with people who need to know Jesus as their Savior.

PSALM 148

Praise the LORD.

Praise the LORD from the heavens, praise Him in the heights above. Praise Him, all His angels, praise Him, all His heavenly hosts. Praise Him, sun and moon, praise Him, all you shining stars. Praise Him, you highest heavens and you waters above the skies. Let them praise the name of the LORD, for He commanded and they were created. He set them in place for ever and ever; He gave a decree that will never pass away.

Praise the LORD from the earth, you great sea creatures and all ocean depths, lightning and hail, snow and clouds, stormy winds that do His bidding, you mountains and all hills, fruit trees and all cedars, wild animals and all cattle, small creatures and flying birds, kings of the earth and all nations, you princes and all rulers on earth, young men and maidens, old men and children.

Let them praise the name of the LORD, for His name alone is exalted; His splendor is above the earth and the heavens. He has raised up for His people a horn, the praise of all His saints, of Israel, the people close to His heart.

Praise the LORD.

HANDS

Isaiah swirled his crook around to catch a sheep by its hind leg. "Absolutely not, Shema. You can't go that way!" His strong, weathered hands pulled the wayward sheep back on the path. "You certainly are stubborn," he told her, picking a burr out of her backside. His leathery hands didn't give way to the bristle's barbs.

When the flock was safely bedded down for the night, Isaiah joined the other shepherds hunched on a hillside with a good view of the area. After another sharp look over his sheep, Isaiah leaned back with his hands behind his head. Everything is so quiet here in Bethlehem, he thought.

Suddenly Isaiah's hands flew up to shield his eyes. Squinting between his fingers, Isaiah saw a blinding light and a figure moving in it. His heart began to pound, and his hands shook.

"Do not be afraid. I bring you good news," the figure said.

Isaiah couldn't take his eyes off the being, though he kept moving his fingers to see if he could see better through the intense light. He listened carefully to the words about the Messiah, born that very day.

Just when Isaiah stopped quivering, thousands more figures appeared. Isaiah fell backward, barking his palms on sharp stones. Thousands of voices were praising Yahweh. It was more beautiful than anything Isaiah had ever heard. In what could have been five minutes or five hours, the bright beings began to grow dimmer, smaller, moving back into heaven. A certain sweetness lingered in the silence.

Slowly Isaiah's hand reached for his staff. The other shepherds moved in dreamlike motions. Isaiah shook himself and looked around. Yes, they saw them, too, he thought.

"What are we waiting for? Let's see this baby!" someone shouted. Along with the others, Isaiah's feet pounded the trail into the nearby village.

A manger was what it said, Isaiah thought. It? It? Those must have been angels! I've seen angels! Thousands of them! And now I will see the Messiah! "Glory! Glory!" Isaiah shouted in his excitement. The others were shouting too.

"Where is a newborn in a manger?" they questioned the townspeople. One old woman pointed to a stable.

Isaiah dashed ahead, arms pumping. He stopped abruptly when he saw a woman leaning over a manger. She looked up, alarmed. Spreading his palms open to show he meant no harm, Isaiah stepped into the stable.

There he saw the tiny newborn. He nudged the baby's hand gently with a finger that suddenly looked huge next to the tiny one. The baby was asleep. The woman and her husband looked tired, too, but Isaiah had to tell them about the angels. His hands danced as he told the story.

Afterwards, Isaiah touched the baby Messiah once more. Kneeling there, he pulled his hands back and clasped them as the wonder of being chosen to know all this overcame him. "I praise You, O Mighty One," he sang in his heart. "I have touched the blessed Lord!"

Make a Christmas Memory

★ There's a song about a poor boy who used his hands to praise Baby Jesus. It's called "The Little Drummer Boy." You might write the lyrics, "Then He smiled at me," on a sign and tape it to the ceiling above your child's bed. It's a benediction your child can look at just after talking to Jesus during evening prayers.

★ Keep track of every hand that touches your front or back door this Christmas season. Trace each hand onto green paper and get the "owner" to sign it. When you're ready, overlap the hands into a wreath. Praise God for what each of these people does for your family.

★ Only a few people have seen angels, and even fewer have seen them in their glorious form. Sprinkle various colors of powdered tempera on foil. Cover with a clean sheet of paper. Trace your idea of an angel streaming with glory with an ice cube on the top sheet. Enjoy the colors!

Look at your hands. In your family prayers, thank God for 10 ways He blesses you through your hands.

CHRISTMAS PEALING

When you hear the word *pealing* you probably think of *peeling* fruit or *peeling* skin from a severe sunburn. But *pealing* spelled with an *a* means something else altogether—something that has to do with bells.

Bells can make all sorts of sounds: tolling, tinkling, clamoring, jingling, chiming, clanging, and pealing. Pealing bells ring out glad shouts of joyful celebration to a town or city by ringing loudly in continuous motion. The Liberty Bell was meant for pealing. Bishop Paulinus of Rome is said to have started the use of pealing bells on Christmas Eve about 1,600 years ago.

Today, many churches around the world use pealing bells at Christmastime. Do you have bells at church or at home?

Make a Christmas Memory

★ Sometimes the clapper of a bell is not inside but outside the bell. Striking any bell-shaped hollow with a dense object will produce a bell tone. A spoon tapped on a drinking glass will work. The old game of lining up glasses filled with varying amounts of water can be entertaining. Tying objects on a clothesline, ready for tapping, gives the effect of playing chimes. Invent your own bell-like instrument and play it to welcome Jesus.

★ Trace or photocopy the bell on page 83. Use it to cut two bells from paper or tagboard. Cut along the dotted line from top to center on one bell and from bottom to center on the other. Slide the bells together along the center cuts. Punch a hole in the top and string a cord through as a hanger.

★ Securely tape a square of plastic wrap onto a table over a picture of bells. (Coloring books or Christmas cards are good sources for pictures.) Outline the bells and color them with permanent markers. Carefully unstick and lift the plastic wrap. Tape the plastic to foil-covered cardboard to make a shining bell. Or tape it to a sunny window!

★ Bells are a fairly modern invention. What other "new" objects help us praise God? You might name synthesizers, CDs, hymnals, and many other things.

· ·

Ring bells as you chant together.

First Reader: Bells tell—
Second Reader: Bells knell—
All: Come and worship!
    Come and worship!

First Reader: Bells ring—
Second Reader: Bells sing—
All: Joy and gladness!
    Joy and gladness!

First Reader: Bells weal—
Second Reader: Bells peal—
All: Christ has come!
    Christ has come!

First Reader: Amen!
Second Reader: Amen!
All: Amen!
    Amen!

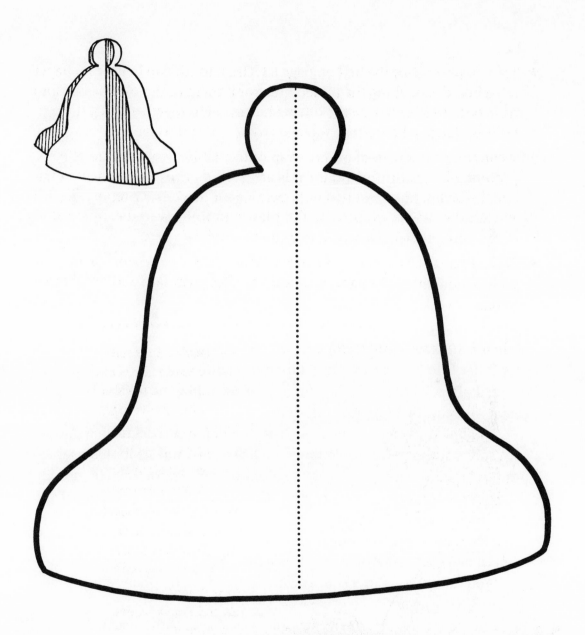

EPIPHANY

"If April gets to do the icing, can I do the gumdrops?" Geof asked.

Mom was just lifting a bundt cake out of the oven. "Yes, but not until the cake cools."

"Do you know where the bean is?" Geof asked.

"I'm not telling," answered Mother with a wink. "It's in there somewhere!" Just then Geof's twin, April, bounded into the kitchen with a crown on her head.

"I bet I find the bean. Then I'll be the Epiphany queen. I already know which game I want us to play, and I'll choose ice cream with chocolate syrup for dessert!"

"If I find the bean," countered Geof, "we'll do a puzzle and have popcorn and rootbeer." Geof took the crown from April and set it on the table next to the Jesus figure they had taken out of their crèche set. He moved the three kings a little closer to Jesus. Geof stared at the scene, puzzled. "We don't have the star, Mom."

"Yes, we do! Yes, we do! Aster showed me. I know where it is!" chanted April in a sing-song voice.

"You can show us after supper when we read the Epiphany story," said Mother. "Now scoot!"

Later, after supper, when the table was clear, Mother carried in the

Epiphany cake the twins had decorated. It looked like a jeweled crown. "Before we slice it and see whose piece has the bean in it for Epiphany king or queen, let's have Aster read from Matthew 2 in the Bible."

Aster got the Bible from the shelf. When she read the part about the star, April started to get up. Mother signaled her to wait. At the end of the reading, Geof asked, "So where is the star?"

"Okay, April," Mother said.

April disappeared into the refrigerator and came back with an apple. "The star is in here!" she said, pointing.

Geof's eyebrows went up. Aster took a knife and cut the apple in half crosswise. Then April held up one slice. "See!" she triumphed. She held it over Jesus, and Geof moved the Wise Men the rest of the way under the seed-star. Everyone watched without a sound. It was almost as if they were with those kings long ago.

Geof broke the spell when his tummy rumbled. Mother chuckled. "I guess somebody's ready for cake!"

Make a Christmas Memory

★ In Europe, children put gold crowns on any pictures or statues of Jesus in the house for Epiphany. January 6 is the day we celebrate the Wise Men visiting Jesus in a little house in Bethlehem. These early astronomers saw the special star God placed in the sky. God led them to find their newborn King.

★ Marzipan is a Christmas candy from Spain that goes well with the jeweled crowns of Epiphany. Boil 1 cup water and 2 cups sugar in a heavy pot to 232°. Remove the pot from the burner and beat the mix until it is slightly cloudy. Add 1½ cups finely ground almonds, ½ cup chopped citron, 2 lightly beaten egg whites, and 1 teaspoon vanilla. Knead on a surface sprinkled with 3 or 4 tablespoons powdered sugar. Roll into balls or cut into squares.

★ Thinking of the gifts Jesus received, your children can make spice-ball pomanders to hang in a cupboard. Poke cloves into an orange and roll in cinnamon. (Using a nail to make each hole before pushing the clove in makes this craft easier.)

★ Make stars from paper ribbon using these directions:

1. Make six loops of ribbon, as shown.

2. Staple each of these ribbons to a center circle of ribbon.

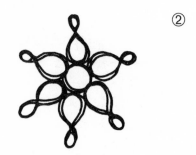

3. Make six loops of ribbon, as shown.

4. Staple these loops between the six star points.

. . . .

Have you ever let God borrow your face so He could smile at someone? You might think about inviting Him to do that every time you walk down a certain sidewalk or hallway.

86

OUR CHRISTMAS PRAYER

Write a prayer with your family that you can pray together before you open your gifts. Thank God for sending His Son, Jesus, as your best Christmas gift.

FAVORITE CHRISTMAS MEMORIES

Describe favorite memories and events from this Christmas season in the Christmas shapes. Date each memory and have family members write their names.

Before writing in these shapes, make several photocopies of these pages. Then you can record years of Christmas memories!

OUR CHRISTMAS GUESTS

Invite guests to describe a Christmas memory at your home.

Name: _____
Date: _____
Christmas Memory: _____
_____
_____
_____

Name: _____
Date: _____
Christmas Memory: _____
_____
_____
_____

Name: _____
Date: _____
Christmas Memory: _____
_____
_____
_____

☆ Name: _____
Date: _____
Christmas Memory: _____
_____
_____
_____

☆ Name: _____
Date: _____
Christmas Memory: _____
_____
_____
_____
_____

☆ Name: _____
Date: _____
Christmas Memory: _____
_____
_____
_____
_____

Name: _____
Date: _____
Christmas Memory: _____
_____
_____
_____
_____

Name: _____
Date: _____
Christmas Memory: _____
_____
_____
_____
_____

Name: _____
Date: _____
Christmas Memory: _____
_____
_____
_____
_____